GHOSTHAWK

Matt Rader

Ghosthawk

NIGHTWOOD EDITIONS

2021

Nightwood Editions
P.O. Box 1779
Gibsons, BC VON 1V0
Canada
www.nightwoodeditions.com

COVER DESIGN: Myron Campbell
TYPOGRAPHY: Carleton Wilson

Nightwood Editions acknowledges the support of the Canada Council for
the Arts, the Government of Canada, and the Province of British Columbia
through the BC Arts Council.

This book has been produced on 100% post-consumer recycled, ancient-forest-
free paper, processed chlorine-free and printed with vegetable-based dyes.

Printed and bound in Canada.

LIBRARY AND ARCHIVES CANADA CATALOGUING IN PUBLICATION

Title: Ghosthawk / Matt Rader.
Names: Rader, Matt, 1978- author.
Description: Poems.
Identifiers: Canadiana (print) 2021024559X | Canadiana (ebook) 20210245603
 | ISBN 9780889714045 (softcover) | ISBN 9780889714052 (HTML)
Classification: LCC PS8585.A2825 G56 2021 | DDC C811/.6—dc23

Contents

Reading Bashō the morning after
Lafayette Square, then speaking
with you on the stairs, a tiny spider
rappelling from your arm.

Gopher Snakes

And long after
my first marriage,
in grassland

beside a turbid creek,
coiled around
canyon cliffs,

two gopher snakes
fucking
in a shallow pit,

dusty, roiled,
oblivious,
the colour of winter

runoff, and us
dead-stopped,
witness.

Lichen

What is this we see
coming into being?
The emulsive sky.

Rain and at the same
time quick-brightening
sun on the horse path

beyond the school
parking lot. Ideograms
for water moiling

light on the blacktop.
You love especially
composite organisms,

lifeforms with properties
very different
from the properties

of their component parts.
I love the gold leaf
burnished in pine bark,

the hillsides lichened
by brassy grasslands,
a dark patina of trees.

Everything is process.
Do you see the latent
shape developing silver

blue on the cloudface?
This is the shade
of all my inchoate

dreams that when I think
on change, mutate,
dissolve into imagery.

Mariposa (1)

Did I say *lonely*?
I meant *lovely*.
I meant the mariposa

lily reminds me,
in colour and shape,
of something

I might kiss,
deeply. I say
desire is a form

of fear. You say
the body
is the soul's way

of summoning
another
soul. Whatever

that means. I think
the foothill
of this mountain

with its community
of lilies
and sagebrush

is inside me
and I'm in
the long afterlife

of History. I think
thinking
about my feelings

rarely helps me
feel differently.
In the cancer ward

where you slept
the curtains were
the pale lilac of the lily.

Houndstongue

After the first example
we couldn't identify
came a second,

a third. Nearby,
an open brook ran clear
through a low fog

of forget-me-nots,
Hitler's favourite flower.
Understand,

a thing named
between two people
cannot be

unnamed. Between
two people
a name will begin

to propagate
in ditches, waste lands.
When we turned

from the third example
at the edge of the path
below the script

of white clematis,
we saw it anew
opposite us,

serious, purple,
the hairy, lance-
shaped language

of its leaves
giving its name over
and over again.

Spring Azure

I love my friends,
I said
over and over

in my head. I saw
a forget-me-not–
coloured butterfly

in stop-motion flutter
over a memorial
ground of white

flowers. Go beyond
your mind,
Jesus said. Beyond

my mind is a gate,
and beyond
the gate is math

and a fractal blue
butterfly blinking
an indecipherable

semaphore
of wings. At the edge
of my dissolving

are those who know
me before my
dissolving. How large

must we grow
before we become
a thing

indistinguishable
from another
thing from the sea,

from the blue sails,
tacking leeward
between the trees.

Ghosthawk

The principal stars
visible
at this hour

have many names.
For example,
Algol,

a.k.a. Demon Star,
from the Arabic
for *demon*

star. This planisphere
was a childhood
gift from a man

who desired
whom he desired
in plague years,

who promised
he'd haunt us as
a hawk when he died,

then died. Now,
ghosthawk is the only
spirit guide

I ever recognize.
Today, the names
of flowers

title all my feelings:
blue flax, morning glory,
goat's beard.

For example, *aster*
from the Greek for *star*.
For example, desire

which is visible, clearly,
at this latitude,
at this hour.

Garlic

You rise from the garden
swinging a bulb
of garlic like a thurible

*

or a lantern. Here is
the small light,
its filament of purple

*

you kept earthed all winter.
A censer, cloven
yet bundled together.

*

Later I peel the skin
from two fleshy moons
and crush them.

*

In the black skillet:
iron, sulphur, oil spitting
like a meteor shower.

*

With a sprig of parsley
between your teeth,
you breathe

*

in my ear, take me
firmly in
your hand.

*

Through the openwork
of your body
comes a pomander

*

of photons and water.
What passes through me
with a shudder: Time,

*

heat, a vision of a star
yanked free from the night,
dirty with loamy sky.

Bitterroot (1)

Work is holy,
my teacher said,
looking out a window

at the empty expanse
of our poems.
Beyond

where he could see,
in the arid, brush steppe
above the city

of Yakima, Washington,
the bitterroot
turned on

its primus of pink
and white light
a few hundred feet

from the interstate.
I'd worked forty years
to see a thing

so perfectly tuned
and burning clear
below a sky's blue flame.

Once, a rattlesnake
the colour of Yakima
earth lifted the ancient,

holy light of her rattle
toward me.
Through the window

in her cage, I watched
the whole desert
undulate

down the hollow,
coiled length
of her body.

Dreamberries

I'm closed-
captioning dreams
no one else can see,

a friend tells me
in a dream
where I show him

the red thimbleberry
and he knows
exactly what I mean—

Along the river
where you
and I stop to breathe,

white linen
handkerchiefs
in pockets

of broad green leaves.
I know it's not enough
to make things

pretty. The dark
steel girder bridging
the river,

its spray-painted
swastika and names.
When I was young

I couldn't breathe
without the help
of a machine

twice a day—
Outside the truck
we watch

the heavy river play
its reel
of sky and trees.

Yarrow

The delicate open-
work of yarrow
knitting

white doilies
among fescue
and ladybirds.

Would you believe me
if I told you
Achilles staunched

battle wounds
with a poultice
of yarrow?

I say the best
orientation
is disorientation.

You say nosebleed,
old man's pepper,
woundwort.

Who wants to
half see, you complain,
the underlying

surface of things?
Who wants
to be without

pain? In the Hebrides
a yarrow leaf held
to the eyes

gave second sight.
From our bent coign
of vantage we see

through the lacy gaps
of flowerhead
airglow, earthlight.

Snowberry

Long before
the first snowfall
snowberries.

While you were
scouting the year's last
forget-me-not

all alone
in the murky
fenland pond,

I was watching
ghosts feed
on the pale flesh

of snowberries.
There's a look
a person gets

when she's
ready for death.
The meadow

didn't have it.
Just sprays of holly
and snowberry

hovering
a few inches above
everything:

bedstraw,
wildrye,
goldenrod,

that shrub
I couldn't name
you called bugbane.

Corpseberry.
To be consumed
by spirits and remain.

Merlin

Conjured from a confetto
of snow, and prestoed
into my apartment window,

*

a flacon of grayscale,
bluish, pale,
sentinelled on the balcony rail,

*

the itty-bitty pigeon hawk,
spellbound, silent,
with a Trappist's eye to talk.

*

Little seer, little revenant,
let me be myself
and myself self-evident.

*

Pinned down but untouched,
I didn't dare move
from my perch on the couch:

*

I'd been visited
by the ghost of the continuous present,
by which I mean *revisited*,

*

or brought back, replenished,
no words, no bullshit,
only here and now, only body-English:

*

the old master
in her cassock of feathers,
charmholder, spellcaster,

*

custodian of the spirit idiom:
You don't have to like everyone,
but you have to love them.

Winter Suns

I saw them
grubbing in the deep
glassy mud

of a cornfield.
The feathery orbs
of their bodies

the colour
of winter suns,
of white breath

lifting off pilings
in the slough.
Hard black

lacquered beak.
Lead-shot eyes.
That line from Yeats

with the staggering girl,
her caressed thighs.
Like hard light,

like the great open
wings of recognition
falling. Filthy,

celestial,
the birds descend
each winter.

I keep coming
back to the valley
I most remember,

my island, the question
that is its own
answer. I saw swans,

then the real
sun moulting
through the milk-blue.

Snow Light

The children
are frozen
around the animal

of night. I slit the belly
and out spills
snow

like winter swans
wicking rain,
like cash money

of an empire
emptied of history,
like all the pale babies

and all the pale dead
drifting slowly
to Earth

again. It's what
you can do with a knife
that big, that sharp

and made
of light. My daughter
receiving the host

of sky on her tongue.
Everything is
sexual. I'm sorry.

I go out into the museum
of darkness
where light performs

as light across the sheets
of snow shrouding
the statuary of homes,

the formless bushes
of shadow and bunch-
grass. I come from

nothing, goes the story
of the night
and the winter,

the riches of the lilac
leaves scattered
like memory,

like conversation.
In the dark,
when I close my eyes

it gets brighter.
I know if the ice crystals
on the blacktop,

the rippling waves
of glass
we call windows, the full

spectrum of light
spilling
from a television set

in a stranger's eyes.
If all you hear
is *I'm sorry*

and *rippling waves*
and *formless shadows.*
The air is self-

healing. That's what
you can do
with a hand that big,

that tender, that can reach
the sky. The alms
of stars,

the purse of moon-
light. All the pale
fractals

drifting crazily.
I'm unfinished,
bewildered

by how far I can travel
away from myself
inside

myself. The three-legged
dog, its stream
of steaming light

in the corner
of the museum
beneath a streetlamp

in pixels of snow. Snow's
memory for footprints,
me walking home

and walking away
from home
past the squat black

shapes of garbage cans
lined up like pawns
along the street,

past the block
of schoolyard
chain-link

quoting the sky
of snowflakes,
in the companionship

of cold, with its thousand
meanings, its luxury
of ice, its thinness

of air, its snow light
that is nothing
hardening

in your hair. I know
if winter swans
in a field of grubs,

if daylight's
children spilling
onto the bleach green

of snow, the eyes
that are rocks,
that outlast

the body,
the jet plane's
undulating cape

of sound passing through
me as nothing
but undulating sound,

the chess pieces
of my daughter's teeth,
her open mouth

collecting
the offerings
of snow,

its poverty, its abundance.
It's what you can do
with an animal

that hungry, that holy,
and composed
of stars. I turn out

the lights. Through
window shadows
I watch snow

move like thought
across the mutable glass,
signal noise

dissolving the edge
of things,
car hood, road verge,

the halo
of the basketball hoop
hovering

above the driveway,
its locution
of capital

and games. If each
disruption
of the pattern

is a new pattern.
The swans battering
air. The face of chaos

in the helix of snow.
If I'm an animal
picking ice

from your hair.
I'm making myself
a blade

out of everything
I see. I'm closing my eyes.
I'm seeing the light.

No thing, a zero in the amber of time, then one.
At the edge of the mind a soft rime: then one.

Jewels of rain like *We'll grow rich with water,*
like every number were prime. Then one.

Storm sky etched by lightning, dissolved by light.
Twelve bodies trenched with lye, then one.

On the horizon, tank columns, shattered sun.
The force of force is two—a rhyme—then one.

Nine grapes eight cancers seven days six fires
five priests four dogs three crimes two, one…

In the meadow of despair grows nothing plus nothing
plus nothing in knots of brooklime. Then one.

From the diamond fire walked the eight legs
of the bodhi spider, numerator, sublime earthen one.

We made love in the corner of the laundromat.
Many deaths. Many lives. Many times. Then one.

Awake in our world, the bird of the liver
alights deep between the lobes. Dreaming,
she rises and together we travel. She hails
from a world previous this world, this body.
An aspect of me before me. Like atoms.
Minerals. Poetry. The bird shudders,
and the toxins in the liver bend my mind
to the flight path of the bird between worlds.
This is how I know the bird survives me.
Like atoms. Poetry. When I'm the bird,

the field of infinite space between every material
thing expands within the body and the body
becomes the flight path of the bird between
worlds. I recall her in the lemon light of a glass
of cider. Nightfall. Winter. The void coming forward
within the void. It's afterimage. From the Greek
for *without protection*. In your own home
with your family over a game of dominoes.
I've awoken to myself time and again, the bird
cold in the cloudland of my liver. I've heard it

whistling all my life. *There are people you love*
whose homes you'll never visit. This is the song
the tuneless bird is singing at the cave
of my birth, in the swollen neighbourhood
of my liver, its projection in the psyche,
an animal shape carrying songs across dimensions.
Like atoms. The black-capped chickadee
motionless on your back step. Its winding sheet
of cotton, its antechamber in the lobes
of the Earth, without protection. Did I say *liver*?

I meant *lover*. I meant the soul is always
a bird, a friend says, casting a shadow
on the Earth, a dark spot on the ultrasound,
a whisper. The liver will regenerate
goes the myth and it's true because, yes,
the bird will open its wings and sail
the hull of the ribs. Between dreams
and waking the animal of my body quivers
like atoms. The body is in many times
at once. It feels so good not to breathe

I panic, your hand around my throat, the bird
singing, *Do not get too close.* Do not close
your eyes. The latent shape on the cloudface.
The mirage of names. The stereo wind
blaring from the source. Your love can be
in many times at once. Your liver in many times.
I love you more than anything, I tell one
daughter. *I love you more than anything,*
I tell the other. Together the bird and I book
passage, a ghostwind whistling between

worlds with each exhalation. The table
of domino bones. The autoinjector dilating me
into total presence, total here-and-now.
The heart of a black-capped chickadee will beat
480 times a minute I remember the radio
telling me. I remember sitting in the back seat
waiting for the corridor of my throat to close
just before we reach the final door. In the cloudland
of plain speaking, the bird is a way of thinking
the unthinkable, what's known without

thought. What's shaped. It survives the air
of the body. It figures. I'm naked. Without
protection. I'm saying what I can say about
living in a body. What we can tell the stars,
their little mouths of light opening and closing,
whistling a tune from a world previous ours.
I'm looking around at instruments, curtains.
Thank you, I say to the second injection
of epinephrine, the line in my arm,
the cloudland of vapour the air compressor

conjures around my head. *You're saving my life*
for later, sang the cold black chickadee
in the flight path of your hands. Later, I don't
recognize pics of me on my phone, face heavy
with fire, eyes whistling the true song
of the liver, its psychotropic toxins, its poison
arrow, its bird, its poetry. I've been dead
before, says the body. I love you more
than anything. In your own home. Without
protection. *I love you*, I said. I love you.

And that is the song this world is singing.
A crown of stars. Their tiny open mouths, a wind
wheezing between lobes. This is where they go,
I tell my children, hands full of dominoes.
Meaning bodies, their joy and inevitability,
our blinkering mass of atoms and poetry,
morning's threadbare hospital gown of sky.
I'll never be able to say everything I want
to say, is what I want, finally, to say. I'm not
special. I'm just here. And here… and here…

The brook was running clear. Now it's gone.
I'm here, cried the killdeer. *I'm here*. Now it's gone.

We built a small house in the womb of the woods.
Twice you gave birth there. Now it's gone.

My name flashed in your mind, the familiar
pale spectre in the mirror. Now it's gone.

I kept one swan, black, in the cameo I wore
around my neck like fear. Now it's gone.

In the dark eye of the night the moon brimmed,
an incandescent tear. Now it's gone.

In the morning, the fever broke like a horse.
All your life: a ringing in the ears. Now it's gone

You held your third finger to the statue's third eye.
In your mouth a ruby appeared. Now it's gone.

Quietly, the maple tree undressed itself at our feet.
We had something, Matt, my dear. Now it's gone.

What Was Coming

We knew what was
coming—the outburst
of green,

the fanfare of needles
and leaves,
and always, eventually,

the copper and auburn,
the russet and ochre
tickertape

reckoning windswept
and eddied
at our doorstep,

like confusion blown clear,
finally, but not
forever, of its origin.

Cedar Waxwing

The exact moment
we reincarnated
as ourselves

behind
the map kiosk
at the trailhead

parking lot,
you pulling up
your pants, me

looking you square
in the back of the head,
there appeared

of summer air,
strange birds
in rakish masks,

bespoke and be-
spoken
in the cloister

of chokecherry.
They flitted and *screed*
between the scrim

of branches
as if nothing
but themselves

had come just then
into flesh,
gobsmacked, agog,

verklempt
to find themselves
returned.

Trembling Aspen

What's here is not
only what interacts
with light,

what I know
of this place, what I can
show. The shimmer

of aspen
in a tipple of wind
that rises now

like evidence
of nothing
that can be

spoken
then falls back again.
The thimblerig

of juncos
in a cup of sun
and shadow. Death is

part of my body.
You can touch it
and do.

But mine
is only one
of many

that are also mine,
said the quaking aspen,
within its quiver

of selves. Here I am
again, and again,
and again.

Moonlight

I didn't think
I could live here.
Neither did you.

The catalpa
with its asterisks
of white bloom

means nothing.
If you're right
and the great pleasure

of jealousy
is to have
your desire

ratified
by the desire
of another

then so what?
Brooklime,
its blue welts

rising
in the flooded lawn.
The jess

of the falcon
that drew its hood
of shadow

over us
while we clutched
each other

in the woods.
A new master.
An old glove.

Yes, you can hear
moonlight
shatter.

Pincushion Mt.

It's true, regret
can circle you
like a slow cyclone

of vultures
wobbling
higher and higher

on expanding air.
What these birds are
searching for

is the scent
of rotting flesh.
Remorse.

I don't want to forget
anything
but the mind

exercises its mercy
despite me.
Now, the committee

for the preservation
of guilt
assembles

in the ponderosa
across the ravine.
Even forgiveness

if we choose
to grant it
to ourselves

can be a loss. Grief
for what we were
never able

to keep. A jury
of vultures feeding
we call a wake.

Lake of the Sun

It's the trace
of damage
that testifies,

hammered-metal
sunlight
on battered water,

the anonymous
bird backlit,
cutting through

for darker passage,
two thin lines
of brightness

streaming
from its shoulders.
I have to tell you:

there's nothing,
in this world
I can't imagine

myself
doing. How
the white light

of midday sun
holds space
for no vision,

how it projects
its glitchy
fragmented glyphs

over the pontoon
bridge. It's like this
and it isn't.

Arrow-Leaf Balsamroot

I was lost. A shadow
covered the sky
like a runner. Then more

shadows, a pack
reeling in
a tired animal.

I closed my eyes.
There, the umber eye
of the balsamroot

looked back,
its arrow leaves
pointing in all directions.

The tired animal
was not the sky,
but the first shadow,

running. Every part
of the balsamroot
is edible,

I told the sagebrush
and the many grasses
gathered around us.

They all knew
about the giant reactor
the balsamroot

modelled its flower on.
My daughter
might have drawn that,

I said, meaning
the bright yellow rays
we call petals,

meaning the sun
bleeding out
across the empty sky.

Yellowthroat (1)

No one knows
what's happening.
The birds

in spring evenings
sound
like lasers sound

in movies.
It's a fact:
no one knows,

most of all
the common
yellowthroat calling

your money,
your money,
your money,

from the half-inked,
half-coloured
sketch of hawthorn

hung haphazardly
in your window
gallery. Art can survive

a market economy,
supposedly,
but it can't survive

outside
your body. A cow-
bird will lay

more than forty eggs
in the nest
of another species.

Such scale, opportunity.
What does this
have to do with me?

Yellowthroat (II)

The answer is
nothing. The forsythia
waves

its yellow flag
at the beady black eye
of the warbler,

and the warbler's
tiny phasers fire
sweet, sweet,

sweet, through
the willows
and thickets. My mind

is only here
to hear
these things

and witness
my hearing. Everything
has a song. My song goes

windhold,
airglow,
earthlight—

That wee yellow-
throat skulking
in bluestem

and feather grass
makes nothing
happen, said the sky

in its measured
prosody of horizons.
Like memory.

Like grief. I pay out
my breath.
It rushes back.

Sagebrush Buttercup

Once there was
nothing. Then this
flower. What is

the cost
of bringing something
so yellow

into being? Imagine
a circle
of infinite radius

and no centre. Now
imagine
this tiny array

of solar power
growing
wild on a western slope

of kinnikinnick
and snowbrush. I'm trying
to describe

the nothing where
I believe
this buttercup

used to be. A circle
within a circle
within. Anoint

Time's arrow
with a poison
made of buttercup's

wild yellow. Show me
the beginning,
middle, beginning

again. Call this
what it is: great love,
great suffering.

Bitterroot (II)

Fear, I kept
repeating
is about something

that hasn't happened
yet. When the sun
let down its hair

over Rose Valley,
the swallowtails
were petals

in strands of light.
That's common beauty
anyone can see.

You have to
be dumb, I think,
to write poetry

when you know,
in the clearing
among the sagebrush,

in a privacy of sun,
the bitterroot
has awoken. *There,*

there, keened
the cicadas, manically,
in their stands

of pine and heat.
This is what is happening,
I thought, always;

I'm not afraid.
*You can do whatever
you want to me,*

offered the stranger
with hair
as opaque as poetry.

Goshawk

What I call ghost
you call goshawk
creeping me

up the creek.
The creek
with its corpus of rock,

its endless
vellum of water.
The rocks

with their pitiless
solitude. The water
with nothing

but the rush
of itself to say.
I've been lucky,

crowed the goshawk
as if he'd forgotten
who he's

supposed to be.
When I forget
who I'm

supposed to be
it's a relief. Even now
the men on the hills

are burning
the autumn slag
because fire, fire,

fire. *Get out of here,*
the goshawk cried,
circling

the white arrow
of its body smaller
and smaller away.

Black Cottonwood

How often I talk
to myself
when I'm alone

in my poems
or walking
between the shadows

of two cottonwoods
I'll never
escape. What powers

the sun is a process,
a sequence,
you say, that yields all

matter. What regret
taught you,
then

desire. Feelings
for people don't change,
you say—

the wind moving
two shadows
across the window—

they just become
something, nameless.
How even now

the cottonwoods loom,
empty, silver.
Through the embrasure

of branches
light falls like arrows
all around me.

Black Mountain

Ohm of the sudden
flash, of heat
lightning

in the mountains.
This is what I resist.
The intimate

gong of thunder
ringing closer
and closer

through the open,
heat-tempered
window

in the psyche. Summer
storms. The crazy
charade

of pin oaks
in a fit of wind.
I've always wanted

things to end
without
ending. The black shelf

of clouds and cloud
shadow. Luminous
flux. As if

change could be
a kind of preservation.
The sine waves

of Time we call
mountains. Frequency.
Amplitude.

What surprises
is what
we already knew.

The Sudden Animal

A shuffling of lake
water, moonlight.
A schpritz of sound.

And unstuck
from the greater
dark, the dark

hunchback
of a beaver
dragging itself

and the wild
like a dim thought
along the shore-

line of City Park.
It came back to me
this evening

reading Bishop's
"The Armadillo"
as you finished

the dishes—
the sudden animal
that's so much

itself it can only be
imagined
as something else.

At first, I didn't know
what it was
gliding half above

half below. Then
I forgot.
The memory

went feral
and comes back now
as it wants.

Red-Osier Dogwood

Lo, in the cave
of fragrance and sun,
I was

of a sudden naked
before myself
and the many

thousands
of candleflames
dappling

the red-osier dogwood
in its altar
of being. No one

laughed. Except
the elderberry
and the goat's beard

and the flickering
creek that held
no reflection,

but continued
to give itself
away without

hesitation. How
do I clean
this mirror

of running water?
I asked the congregation,
which was

the sky in its blue-
white vestments
of oxygen,

which was the red-
osier dogwood,
its ministry of silence.

Lightwell

The morning after you
left, the sun
was a dim white light

that didn't make me
think of anything,
not angels,

not death. I couldn't
look directly
at it

but its effects
were everywhere:
the swarm of raindrops

alive in the lilac,
the metallic skyscape
floating

in my truck's silver paint.
A brightness too bright
to look at

is the true definition
of a thing
beyond me, a white hole

I fall endlessly through
into my body.
Woe, to see the sun,

someone once wrote,
and not think
of angels,

but I'd like to
not think
at all, if possible. Just feel

something cosmic
reach through the altostratus
and touch me.

Mariposa (ii)

Now, the familiar
thunder of questions.
Now, again, the lily.

*

The more I breathe
the less I have
to say

*

about the mariposa,
it's smelter
of water and light

*

turning absence
into a shape
we name

*

lily, turning purple
into the ghost
of last year's

*

petals, turning
petals into three-
part sky.

*

Or, the more I breathe
the more I have
no choice.

*

Or the only thing
turning was the eye
of the lily.

*

Who comes back
exactly
as they were? The lily,

*

its brief equanimity.
Taketh my hand.
Have mercy.

I Was So Happy

Goodbye, the arnica
cried, spinning its wheel
of yellow light

so quickly it appeared
to vanish, then
reappear,

then vanish, then—
In the diamond
air, the undulating green

of the forest whelmed
and whelmed, as if
being born

a million times without
death, without
end. *Whose dream*

is this? is something
I ask when I dream. If I can
see my thoughts,

can you see the owl
heap up
in the high shadow

of the pine tree
where he observes me
observing

my thinking? Let's re-
collect the arms
of the owl, which can be

his wings in their many
notions of geometry,
which can be

the branches of trees.
I was nothing, once.
I was so happy.

Joyland

I want to tell you
something funny,
something true.

Along my street
honey locust trees
burn their autumn

stores of sunlight.
I know
it's not funny.

I'm thinking
of joy
this evening, walking

across the glowing
embers of leaves,
how difficult

it can be
to confront
unabashed sincerity,

when, as if
pranked
into Being, the antic,

black humour
of a bat
bursts like laughter

right in front of me.
It's not funny,
I hear

the honey locusts say.
But I can't stop.
I'm afraid

I might crack
into flame. What's funny
is how perfectly

a honey locust
stores energy
from outer space

then drops it
like burning shadows
at our feet,

or how a bat can
origami
evening air

into its own image
and send it
hurtling

through darkness,
possessed,
wingèd, composed

of ever-changing
shapes. What's true:
the torch-path

of autumn trees,
the ricochet
of bats and laughter,

my joy, its wild
excess. All my life
it's been

easier to talk
suffering
than the weightless

plenitude of grace.
I give you now
the face

of the sun
in a diaspora of leaves,
the shadows

of houses gathering
like people
around a fire,

the bat of laughter
under the lamp-
light of trees

flipping
pages of reality—
Outside

the crummy motel
in Ocean Beach
the sun

claws across
shit-white rocks,
sandy tarmac,

the knit-fringe
of surf you skirt,
barefoot,

your wild blue kite
tugging at you,
making letter-shapes

in the sky,
an athletic, enigmatic
skywriting

whose spirited,
heady sense
you sense clearly

in the taut kite string,
a quivering
line of gravity

through your body
to the centre
of all things.

Acknowledgements

I respectfully acknowledge the syilx / ʔuknáqin people on whose traditional and unceded territory I wrote these poems.

Earlier versions of some poems appeared in *The Walrus*, *Grain*, *Vallum*, *Meltdown 2020*, *The Lonely Voice* (UK), *The Scores* (UK), *EcoTheo* (US), *Terrain.org* (US) and *The Penny Dreadful* (IE). Thank you to the editors of each. "Garlic" appeared as a video poem in the 2021 Seedy Saturday Video Conference proceedings.

I gratefully acknowledge the support of the Canada Council for the Arts and the University of British Columbia.

"Spring Azure" remembers my teacher, Patrick Lane, and my friend, Elise Partridge.

To Darren Bifford, Eduardo Corral, Geri Doran, Erin Hiebert, Cornelia Hoogland, Chris Hutchinson, Emily Lewis, Cole Mash, Amber McMillan, Peter Morin, Tarn Painter-Mac-Arthur, Harold Rhenisch, Erin Scott, Jordan Scott, Michael V. Smith, Russell Thornton, Hayden Ward and Jan Zwicky: I showed you the red thimbleberry; you told me what it meant.

Thank you to Myron Campbell for dreaming up the cover. And to Andreas Rutkauskas for lending photos to dream with.

To Michael Schulting who loves dreams and who guided me, often without either of us knowing.

Thank you to Silas White, Carleton Wilson and everyone at Nightwood.

As always, my family.

About the Author

Matt Rader is the author of five volumes of poetry, a collection of stories and a book of non-fiction. He teaches Creative Writing at the University of British Columbia Okanagan and lives in Kelowna, BC.

PHOTO CREDIT: ERIN STODOLA

The ragged queue of shoppers
in the supermarket parking lot.
In the brook beside the canyon path,
forget-me-nots, buttercups.